The Wild West in American History

PIONEERS

Written by Leonard J. Matthews
Illustrated by Geoffrey Campion and others

Library of Congress Cataloging-in-Publication Data

Matthews, Leonard, 1920-
  Pioneers.

  (The Wild West in American history)
  Summary: Examines the reasons for the westward migration of the
nineteenth century and chronicles the experiences of the men and
women who traveled to the vast western areas of North America and
established farms, ranches, towns, and cities.
  1. Frontier and pioneer life—West (U.S.)—Juvenile literature.
2. Pioneers—West (U.S.)—History—Juvenile literature. 3. West
(U.S.)—History—Juvenile literature. 1. Frontier and pioneer
life—West (U.S.) 2. Pioneers. 3. West (U.S.)—History]
I. Rourke, Arlene, 1944-   . II. Title. III. Series.
F596.M336   1988   978   87-20794
ISBN 0-86625-362-9

Rourke Publications, Inc.
Vero Beach, Florida 32964

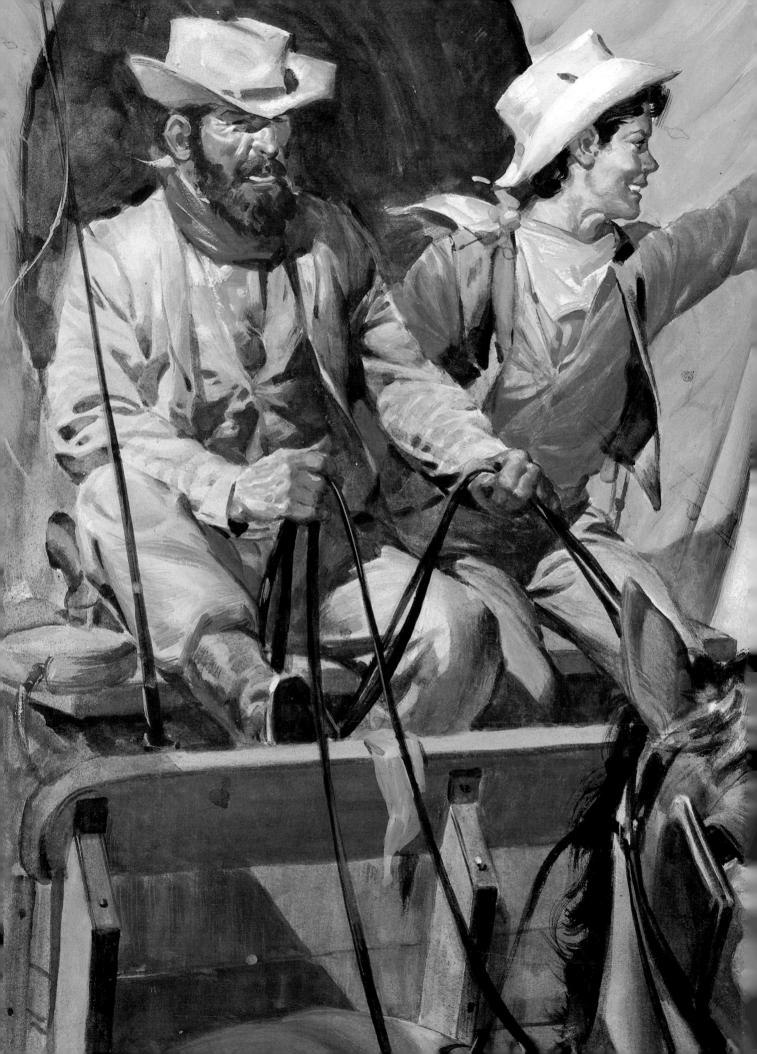

The Wild West in American History

PIONEERS

PIONEERS

People came to the American West for different reasons. Some came looking for gold, and others were running away from trouble. But most people came because they wanted land.

In Europe and in the eastern section of North America, the good farming land was already being used. More and more people wanted new land on which to settle. They wanted somewhere to plant crops, raise stock and start families. They were looking for a new home.

About 150 years ago, thousands of people moved westwards from the Mississippi to settle in the vast western areas of North America. They tamed a wilderness and established farms and ranches, towns and cities. Without these settlers America would not be the country it is today.

The pioneers were not the first white men to travel in the West. Explorers and hunters had traveled across these wide-open spaces. They had met Indians and made maps of the country they crossed.

By 1840 some white men had traveled through the West. There were so few of them, however, that the West was virtually untouched. The pioneers would change all that.

PREPARING FOR THE JOURNEY

Scouts who knew the way West would guide the wagon trains across the deserts and over the high and dangerous mountains.

The pioneers moved west by several routes, or trails, and in several waves. The first important wave of settlers was that which moved along the Oregon Trail in 1843.

This was the largest of the early movements of settlers. In many ways the pioneers traveling the Oregon Trail were typical of many later settlers. It is worth telling their story in full.

The move to Oregon began in the 1830s. Many old mountain men and traders who worked for the Hudson's Bay Company, a large British fur company, retired in those years. Rather than move east, the retired men began farming in the Willamette Valley in Oregon Territory. The climate and land there were very similar to those in Europe. Farming was easy.

At about the same time Jason Lee, a minister, set up a mission in the Willamette Valley. In 1838, after some time in the valley, he traveled

East. He needed extra money to keep his mission going. Traveling through the eastern states, he gave lectures and collected money. Everywhere he went, Lee told people about the beautiful Willamette Valley and how easy it was to farm there.

The people of the East were excited. Many of them were looking for new land to farm. The land described by Jason Lee sounded ideal. Many people decided to move to Oregon to start a new life. In 1843, the first wagon train to arrive in Oregon complete with its wagons left Missouri. The guide was Marcus Whitman, and the immigrants numbered nearly 1,000. A wagon train with 100 people in tow had left Missouri in 1842, but the wagons were abandoned in the mountains.

The farmers reached Oregon safely and settled down to a life of farming. Other people in the East were encouraged by the success of this first wagon train. In 1844, hundreds of people decided to make the journey. Over the following years, several thousand people would follow the Oregon Trail across the plains. Their journey was never easy.

Most of the wagon trains started from Independence, a town in Missouri. Any farmer and his family wanting to travel to Oregon would come to Independence in April or May. Wagon trains always set off in spring so that they would reach Oregon before winter. For two months each year Independence became a hive of activity.

The journey was long and tiring. Each family knew it had to take everything that it might need on the long trail. Farmers had to take all the equipment they needed to start a farm. This was why the pioneers traveled in covered wagons. They carried all their farm equipment in the wagons. Many families also took several head of cattle or horses with them to start herds.

When the pioneers arrived in Independence they would get ready for the long journey ahead of them. First, they had to make sure that they had the right equipment. The most important equipment was the wagon which would carry the farmer, his family, and his tools. Most pioneers had a covered wagon like those seen in movies. There were, however, several dif-

An old engraving of Independence as it was in the early days of the pioneers.

ferent types of covered wagons.

In the early years many pioneers traveled in the same farm wagons that they had used at home. These were strong and could carry everything a

Wagon trains assembled in the town of Independence and prepared for the journey ahead.

pioneer wanted in his new home. Unfortunately, they were not designed for the long journey to Oregon. Many broke down on the way.

Later pioneers used different types of wagons built specially for the difficult journey across the West. The most familiar of these was the prairie schooner, or Conestoga wagon. It was about 25 feet long and had four wheels. A canvas covering swept upwards at either end. Pioneers tried to make sure that the bodies of the Conestogas were watertight. This would mean that they could float across rivers as if they were small boats.

A later type of wagon, used in Canada, was the Red River wagon. This was smaller than the Conestoga. The big advantage of the Red River wagon was that it did not use any metal in its construction. The wagon was made entirely of wood and could be easily repaired if it broke down. Like the Conestoga, the Red River also had a canvas cover. This kept everything inside dry when it rained and stopped the wind from blowing sand into the stores.

Before starting on their journey, the pioneers would make sure that the wagons were in perfect condition. Independence was the home of many blacksmiths. Everybody who visited the town during those pioneer years noticed there were far more blacksmiths than anywhere else. The blazing forges glowed late into the night and the clanging of hammers sounded around the clock.

The first pioneers used oxen to pull their wagons. Oxen moved only two miles each hour. However, they did not tire easily and were able to pull wagons all the way to Oregon.

Most wagons were pulled by either 6 or 8 oxen. When Oregon was reached the pioneers used the oxen to pull plows. Later pioneers, who did not need to travel such a long distance, used horses to pull their wagons. Horses could move faster and could be used for many different purposes once the journey was over.

Inside the wagon were the tools for working a farm. Wood for handles could be found in Oregon, so pioneers often carried only the metal parts of tools, such as axes, shovels and plows. Home utensils, such as saucepans, lanterns,

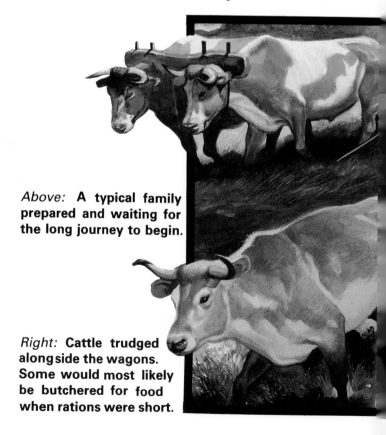

Above: **A typical family prepared and waiting for the long journey to begin.**

Right: **Cattle trudged alongside the wagons. Some would most likely be butchered for food when rations were short.**

bedding, and perhaps a few luxuries, were carried in the wagon. Buckets were hung underneath.

The pioneers also took other objects needed on the journey. These included spare parts for the wagons and food. The average wagon carried 150 pounds of flour and 15 pounds of coffee as well as other food. This would be enough to feed a family on the journey. Often, though, food ran out. The pioneers also took tents, because the wagons were so laden with equipment that they had to sleep outside.

Most of these tools and supplies could be bought in Independence. There were many shops in town which sold necessities to pioneers. During the years when it was the starting point for wagon trains, Independence was one of the busiest towns in America.

All pioneers carried guns. The early Oregon pioneers carried the single-shot pistols and rifles which were then available. Only later did pioneers carry revolvers and repeating rifles. These guns were not invented until later in the century.

THE FIRST FEW DAYS

With their wagon in top condition and enough supplies for the journey, the family's next step was finding a wagon train to join.

There were so many people in Independence that a family would have little trouble finding a wagon train. Generally speaking, all the families ready to leave at the same time would form a train.

There were many advantages to traveling in wagon trains. First of all, Indians and outlaws were unwilling to attack a large number of people.

Most of the benefits were more down to earth. If a family were traveling on its own, no one would be around to help them. If the wagon broke down, the family would be stuck in the middle of nowhere. In a large wagon train, however, there were lots of men to help fix a broken wagon. Perhaps one of them would be a blacksmith who could repair metal parts.

If a wagon could not be fixed, the pioneer family could divide their goods and stores into small amounts. These were then loaded into a number of other wagons. In this way the family would still arrive in Oregon with their equipment. Pioneers depended on each other a great deal during the long journey.

Once a wagon train was assembled, the pioneers would find a guide. Since none of the pioneers knew the way to Oregon, nor did any suspect what the journey would be like, each wagon train had to find an experienced guide.

Luckily there were plenty of men who did know the way. Mountain men and traders had been traveling in the West for a number of years. For these hardened frontier men, guiding a wagon train was an attractive idea. It was easier than trapping beaver or trading with Indians, and it paid well. Many tough frontiersmen could be found in Independence in the spring, each looking for a wagon train to guide.

It did not take long for a wagon train to find a guide. Fees were agreed to in advance. Usually the guide insisted that everyone in the train had to do exactly as they were told. Guides knew the dangers of the journey. Although an order from the guide might seem pointless to a pioneer, it was usually a sensible precaution. If one pioneer disobeyed the guide, the whole wagon train might be placed in danger. Most people were happy to do what the guide told them. Disagreements were rare.

When everything was ready, the wagon train set out from Independence. Most wagon trains left in May. There were very good reasons for this. First of all, the pioneers had to reach Oregon in time to build homes before winter arrived. On the other hand, the pioneers could not leave too early. They had to wait until the grass began to grow on the plains. Each wagon train had hundreds of oxen, cattle and horses

Many difficulties arose when a wide river was reached. At times the pulling of the wagon through the mud could take hours and at the River Platte many would-be pioneers turned back.

with it. There had to be enough grass on the plains to feed all these animals.

The first five days or so were fairly easy. The wagons rumbled across a gentle landscape which held few dangers. These were the 50 miles northwest to the Platte River. During these days, the guide got to know the pioneers in his train. The pioneers learned to accept the orders of their guide. It was a time when everybody became used to traveling together and to the routine of the march.

After 50 miles the pioneers reached the Platte River. This was a very wide, shallow river. One traveler noticed how much mud was in the Platte. He said it was "too thick to drink and too thin to plow."

Crossing the Platte was the first major event on the Oregon Trail. It could be dangerous. On the whole, the Platte was so shallow that the wagons could be driven across. However, there were hidden holes in the river bed. If a wagon fell into one of these, it might get stuck. Many hours could be spent trying to salvage a wagon. If a man fell into a hole or lost his footing, he might be swept away and drowned. Crossing the Platte was far from easy.

Once they had crossed the Platte, the pioneers were truly in wild country. It was the land of the Indians and the buffalos. It was at this point that the journey really began.

A photograph showing wagons crossing a river. Not all the rivers were as shallow as this one.

ON THE PLAINS

During the six weeks which it took to cross the plains, a daily routine was established. Everybody would wake up at dawn, about four o'clock in the morning. They would then cook breakfast and strike camp. This involved taking down any tents, collecting the tools used overnight, and packing everything into the wagons.

Meanwhile the animals had to be rounded up. The oxen and other livestock would have been turned loose to graze the previous evening. Though men would have been keeping an eye on them, some animals might have wandered a distance from the camp. The pioneers had to separate their own oxen from the rest. The men then hitched the oxen to the wagons. They made a last check to be sure that nothing had been left behind. Then they were ready.

About three hours after sunup, the wagon master would give the word to move. Wagons usually traveled in single file. Each wagon would follow in the path of the one before it.

This meant that only the front wagon had to worry about avoiding obstacles. The rest of the train just followed. Also, it was an easy task to persuade the oxen to follow other oxen.

The oxen pulled the wagons at about two miles per hour. Because the wagons were so loaded with stores and equipment, there was little room for people. Only the sick or immobile were allowed to ride in the wagon. Most pioneers walked beside the oxen. One member of the family would lead the oxen forwards. The others would help control the spare horses and the cattle. Some people might just stroll beside the wagon train.

Sometimes men who were good shots would ride separately from the wagon train. They would be looking for animals to hunt since pioneers did not take any meat with them. The only way to get meat was for hunters to go out and find it. Usually these hunters shot buffalo. They would butcher the animal on the spot and then carry the meat back to the wagon train.

Usually the wagon train would stop at noon for a short break. The pioneers would sit down for a rest. Perhaps they would eat a light meal. The animals would be allowed to graze. When the wagon master gave the word, the wagons would move forwards once again.

A few hours before dark, the wagon master would select a camp site and order the train to stop. If the wagon trains were to reach Oregon

in time, they had to travel twelve miles a day, sometimes less. Exactly how far they traveled each day depended largely on the terrain.

Setting up camp was a fairly complicated procedure. First of all, the wagons were arranged in a rough circle. This was a good defense against attack by Indians. The oxen were unhitched and allowed to graze on the rich plains grass. Then beds were made and cooking fires started.

Out on the plains there was no wood to burn. Instead, the pioneers burned lumps of what they called "prairie coal." In fact, these were dried buffalo droppings. Though not as good as wood, prairie coal could be made to burn fairly easily and produced a very good flame. Some of the stores brought in the wagons and meat shot by the hunters would be cooked for the evening meal.

Sometimes, if the pioneers were in a good mood, they might hold a dance. These dances did not last long into the night because everybody had to be on the move early the next morning.

Pioneers needed to provide entertainment and most evenings something was organized.

There was usually somebody in the wagon train who had brought a banjo or other musical instrument. There might be a good storyteller, or someone who had been to or come from Europe. These people would sit and talk while others gathered around to listen.

The plains across which the wagon trains traveled were the home of Indian tribes. Some of these tribes, such as the Sioux, Kiowa, and Comanche, have become famous. Many western films show wagon trains being attacked by Indians. Stories abound of hordes of whooping Indians galloping around circles of wagons, shooting arrows at the pioneers.

In truth this did not happen often. Pioneers were armed with rifles and pistols. Attacking a large group of men and women armed with guns would have been foolish. Indians usually did not bother. When the Indians did attack, however, they were a very real danger.

When the first wagon trains crossed the plains, the Indians were curious rather than hostile. The only white men the Indians had seen before the 1840s had been occasional trappers and traders. They had never seen so many whites at one time.

At night, wagons were arranged in a circle. This was a good defense against an attack by Indians.

Luckily, many of the wagon masters could speak Indian languages. They explained to the Indians that the pioneers did not want to cause trouble. All they wanted to do was to shoot a few buffalo for food and then move on. Once the Indians realized this, they left the wagon trains alone.

The early wagon trains ran into little trouble. Sometimes the Indians might try to steal horses or cattle. Occasionally, a fight might break out if a pioneer caught an Indian stealing or if an Indian felt he had been insulted. On the whole, the early wagon trains rarely fought the Indians. That trouble began later.

After several weeks the wagon trains reached Fort Laramie, or Fort John as it was called until 1849. There the wagon master allowed the pioneers to stop for a few days. The· pioneers would rest and wash their clothes. If the wagons needed repairing, work could be carried out in the workshops of Fort Laramie. After this short break, the wagons headed towards the mountains.

THE MORMON EPIC

he Mormons are a religious sect which was founded in New York State in 1830. There were thousands of converts, and Mormon communities soon sprung up in many areas. Mormon beliefs angered many people. Under their leader, Brigham Young, they sought a new life in the West in 1846.

The wagon train that set out was the largest ever seen. It contained 12,000 people. It wintered in what is now Nebraska. Brigham Young rode ahead to find a place for his people to settle. Reaching a broad valley south of the Oregon Trail, Young said, "This is the place." The Mormons poured into the valley. Within years the wilderness had been transformed into fertile farmland.

The settlement centered around Salt Lake City, a town built by the Mormons in an amazingly short time. The whole of the Salt Lake Valley became an outpost of white civilization. It was hundreds of miles from the next settlement of whites. The Mormons had found what they were looking for: a country of their own.

Thousands of people heading for California stopped off at Salt Lake City. There, settlers in wagon trains could buy supplies and rest. Over the years, many settlers arrived who were not Mormons. Despite this, the area remained a stronghold of Mormonism. In 1896, the Mormon settlement became the state of Utah.

CROSSING THE MOUNTAINS

est of Fort Laramie, the Oregon Trail climbed to cross the Rockies at South Pass. In many ways the mountains were the most difficult part of the journey. The oxen had to drag the heavy wagons up steep hills for mile after mile. If the wagon train arrived late in the year, the pioneers had to cope with deep snow and ice.

The terrain made travel very difficult. Wagon trains were slow. The rocky ground broke many wheels and axles. If the wagons could not be fixed they had to be abandoned. Sometimes a wagon would run out of control and careen down a hill. When it crashed into the rocks at the bottom of a hill, the wagon

would be destroyed and many stores and tools would be lost. Many animals died on this stretch of the journey.

After crossing the South Pass, the wagon trains had a choice. They could either strike directly northwest or take a much longer route to the south. The shorter route had the disadvantage of being more difficult and without water holes. Pioneers usually only took this route if they were late. The longer route passed through better country. The two routes rejoined at Fort Hall on the Snake River.

The wagon trains then followed the Snake River for many miles. The Oregon Trail finally reached the Oregon River near Walla Walla. The official trail wound down the river to the Pacific Ocean. However, most pioneers never reached the sea. Instead, they turned south along the Willamette Valley or one of the other valleys.

Here the pioneers staked out their land claim. They finally unloaded their wagons for the last time and began their farms. Houses were quickly built to protect farmers during the winter. Land was cleared and made ready for planting in the spring. The long journey was over and the new land had been found!

Wagon trains rolled along the Oregon Trail for many years. In some places the passing of thousands of wagons cut such deep ruts that they can still be seen today. Many descendants of these pioneers still live in Oregon.

Pioneers, riding back to find some wagoners who had failed to keep up with the wagon train, would sometimes find their friends killed by Indians.

LATER SETTLERS

The American Civil War virtually halted all settlement in the West. While war raged in the eastern states, no one was eager to set out westwards. As soon as the war was over, however, the wagon trains began rolling again.

In some ways the post-war wagon trains were very similar to the earlier ones. In other ways they were very different. Physically, a wagon train of the 1860s and 1870s looked like those that had rumbled along the Oregon Trail in the 1840s. It was made up of Conestogas covered with white canvas. Everyone traveled in single file, and everyone obeyed the wagon master.

After the Civil War there were far more wagon trains. They moved across the plains in almost unbelievable numbers. Wagon train followed wagon train. More and more settlers arrived in the West.

The big rush of pioneers to the West was spurred by the Homestead Act of 1862. This act offered 160 acres of land in the West to anybody who went there and claimed it. All a man had to do was farm the land for five years and it was his. With the irresistible offer of free land, the settlers flooded westward.

New settlers did not stay on the Oregon Trail. They began to follow other trails to new areas of settlement. One of the most famous of these was the Santa Fe Trail. This route had been used since 1823 by traders and people traveling to Mexico. Now it was being used by wagon trains. Settlers moved along the Santa Fe Trail looking for good farmland that had never been farmed before.

All this angered the Plains Indian tribes. Instead of passing through, the wagon trains were stopping on Indian land. Settlers were beginning to farm on land previously inhabited by Indians. Even worse, from the point of view of the Indians, the settlers killed many more buffalo. Herds of these huge beasts were shot for food. Many more were killed to clear farmland. Professional buffalo hunters later slew thousands of the animals for their hides and tongues only. The Plains Indians relied on the buffalo. Slowly Indians began to realize the threat of the settlers.

Even before these mass emigrations, trouble had begun. In 1861, Cochise led the Apaches of Arizona on the warpath. In 1862, the Sioux attacked settlements on the edge of the plains at New Ulm, now in Minnesota. Hundreds of whites were killed before the Sioux were defeated about a year later.

From that time onward, warfare flared up and died down on the plains. In peace or war, the Indians remained a potential threat. Groups of young Indian warriors often carried out raids when they were meant to be at peace. To further complicate matters, a wagon train of settlers could not be expected to know which tribes were friendly and which were hostile. The settlers had to be on their guard with all Indians.

Wagons were formed into circles every night and lookouts stayed awake all night in case of attack. Still, Indians hesitated to attack wagon trains. They knew that the large numbers of armed men in a typical train would be able to beat off an Indian attack.

Stragglers were a different story. If a wagon fell behind the main train for some reason, it could be in terrible danger. When Indians saw an isolated target, they would pounce. A lone wagon stood little chance against an attack. Burned out wagons surrounded by arrow riddled bodies became depressingly familiar on the western plains. Men taking horses to water would be killed and their horses stolen.

These attacks were often more of a nuisance than a danger. Most wagon trains were safe from attack. The wagon master just had to make sure that his train took all possible precautions against attack.

In 1869, the transcontinental railroad was completed. Settlers had a new and better way of reaching the West. They could take the train deep into the plains. Only then would they take to the wagons and set off to find a piece of land.

By the end of the 1880s, the Indians were no longer a menace. The settlers could go where they wanted to in reasonable safety. In the search for new land, pioneers came westwards in large numbers and by many methods. Some

Rafts would have to be built at dangerous rivers and rapids.

**A pioneer's wife prepares
a hasty meal.**

traveled by railroad. Some came by wagon. Still others loaded their goods on rafts and traveled along rivers. This practice took place in the East and Midwest.

The years between the Civil War and the end of the century were the heyday of the pioneers. Even though pioneers could now reach their lands more quickly and safely, trouble was never far away. Starting a farm or ranch from scratch was no easy matter, as many pioneers learned the hard way.

SETTLING DOWN

When the pioneers of the 1840s reached the end of the Oregon Trail, they found a land very much like that which they had left. The Willamette Valley was a pleasant land of forests and meadows.

After they arrived, the first thing the settlers did was find a place for their farms. Each man was allowed to claim 640 acres of land. Naturally he wanted to find the best 640 acres he could.

Each farm would need to include a section of river or stream. This would provide water for the farmer and his livestock. The stream might also be needed to irrigate the crops. The farmer would also want to include some meadowland, which would be useful grazing for his animals. He would also need an area of woodland to supply him with building materials and firewood. Luckily there was plenty of such land in the Willamette Valley and surrounding areas.

Of course, the local Indians had a great deal of contact with the white settlers. Some tribes were friendly, others were hostile. Whenever Indians were seen approaching, the farmer would arm himself. He could not afford to take chances.

Most settlers arrived in the early autumn. The first thing they did was to build a house. Often several families would join together to build the houses. Trees would be felled and logs shaped for building. Men from several families would join in to build houses in turn. In this way the buildings could be finished more quickly.

As settlements extended along the valleys, Indians became more and more hostile. Eventually, raids gave way to full-scale war. Log cabins were attacked by hostile Indians and settlers were killed or forced to flee. Eventually, the Indians were brought under control, not always by the most humane methods. Only then could the farmers of the far Northwest settle down to taming the landscape.

Farmers encountered many natural problems. Trees had to be cut down to clear land for crops, and marshy ground had to be drained. Grizzly bears and other wild animals had to be kept off the land. Despite these hardships, the settlers in the Oregon country managed very well. Within a few years the land was a patchwork of farms and settlements.

Farmers had to irrigate their fields with water from streams and rivers. This meant long periods of digging to create water channels. Along with the grain fields, there were gardens. Here the farmer's wife would raise vegetables for her family. These too needed constant work and water to produce a good crop.

Most settlers had some livestock. There might be a horse and a few head of cattle. These could be grazed on the open land near the farm or on rich meadowland within the farm.

Occasionally Indians would arrive at the farm. Usually they were friendly. Pilfering by Indians was not uncommon, and neither was horse stealing. Sometimes a full-scale war might erupt. Settlers would have to scurry for protection within the nearest fort. If they could not reach the fort in time, settlers faced death or hideous torture.

One of the biggest problems for the early plains settlers was the loneliness. The flat landscape stretched endlessly to the horizon. It could be miles to the next farm and a day's journey to anything which could be called a town. Apart from their own families, people could go for weeks without seeing anybody. If anything went wrong, there would be nobody to help.

The absence of people was too much for some settlers. They broke down and fled back East. Others thrived on the isolation and built up prosperous holdings.

Later pioneers who came to live on the plains had to cope with very different problems. Perhaps the most immediate problem for farmers on the plains was the lack of wood. How could farmers build houses without wood? The answer was the sod house.

Some trees grew along the banks of rivers on the plains. Timber cut from these trees was used to build a frame for a house. Then the farmer would set to work cutting pieces of turf, or sod, from the prairie. These were piled up against the wooden frame to form the walls and often the roof as well. These sod houses were surprisingly successful. They could be built quickly and cheaply. During the winter the sods kept in the heat of a stove. The summer

Log shacks could always be built at journey's end but the settlers had to be ready for the approach of hostile Indians.

sun beat down on sod roofs, which provided welcome shade.

With his house built, the settler could start farming. It might seem that the plains settler had an easier task than the settler in the Oregon country. He did not have to fell trees to clear land for crops. In fact, he faced a hard time getting started.

The soil on the plains was tough and difficult to plow. A farmer needed all his determination to turn his free 160 acres into a viable farm. Furthermore, the climate was a problem. The plains were much drier than the eastern lands where the pioneers had grown up. Rarely could fields of grain be planted and then expected to grow. In a wet year, wheat might grow easily. Most years, however, the wheat would sprout and then dry out and die before it was ripe.

As the numbers of people on the prairies in-

Once settled and their sod house built, the pioneers had to work hard on land that was not always very productive.

Grandfather and all his family pose for a photograph outside their sod house.

creased, new problems emerged. Before the farmers arrived on the western plains, the land had been taken over by the cowboys. With the plains swept clean of Indians and buffalo, the vast grasslands had been empty.

Enterprising ranchers moved in with herds of cattle. Within a short time hundreds of thousands of cattle were roaming the plains. Nobody owned the land on which the cattle grazed. Ranchers just turned their cattle loose on the open range and cowboys kept track of the cattle. The cattle of each ranch were branded to show who owned them.

When the first farmers began to arrive, the ranchers did not mind. If anything, they welcomed the farmers because it gave the cowboys people to talk to. If the farmer had a daughter, she might even marry a cowboy.

When the numbers of farmers increased, things changed. When a farmer arrived, he naturally wanted to settle on the best piece of land he could find. Except for the land of other settlers, none of the land belonged to anybody. The newcomer would choose a site on the

banks of a river and stake out his land.

After a time, the farms of the settlers could be found running along the banks of the rivers. This began to annoy the ranchers. They were used to their cattle roaming at will across the prairies. Disputes began to take place over water. Farmers were settling on the same river banks that cattle used as watering holes. When the cattle could no longer drink at the rivers, they began to die of thirst.

The farmers might have had a legal title to their patch of land, but the ranchers had got there first, and they had the guns to prove it. Several pioneers who refused to leave the farms were found shot dead. Others simply disappeared. At times the cowboys were the ones found dead. Such feuding occurred throughout the West. It cost the lives of many men and women but rarely erupted into major outbreaks of violence.

Perhaps the most famous of all range wars was the Johnson County War. By 1891 the ranchers of Johnson County, Wyoming, had had enough of farmers taking over prairie land. They hired 52 gunmen to blast the farmers off the range. In the violence which followed, the farmers defeated the gunmen.

Added to that, in 1886-87 a particularly savage winter killed thousands of cattle. Many ranchers went bankrupt. The plains now belonged to the farmers.

CIVILIZATION COMES TO THE PLAINS

Farmers and their families had always missed the civilized comforts of life in the East. When there were only a few pioneers earning a living on the soil, it was impossible to establish the civilization for which they longed. As numbers increased, however, so did the ambitions of the farmers.

The first sign of a maturing society was the appearance of towns. These towns could be strange places. Sometimes they were little more than a collection of shacks. Farmers from the surrounding prairie would come to town to meet and talk. There would normally be a store where farmers would buy supplies and equipment, and a saloon where they could meet for a drink and catch up on the latest news. Perhaps there would also be a blacksmith to help repair metal tools.

As railroads spread across the West, a new kind of town began to spring up. It was the railroad town. In many cases railroad towns were similar to the earlier shack towns. In addition to the other stores, they had a railroad station, and often a telegraph office. This meant that they were in contact with the outside world. Goods and equipment could be shipped in by train. The crops raised by the farmers could be sold to the railroad. A town with a railroad was always a larger and richer place than one without a railroad.

As more and more farmers moved on to the prairies, towns grew larger. They came to be the centers for a countryside full of farmers. Towns might now number a few hundred people. There would be several stores. Many services were available: blacksmiths, launderettes, hotels, saloons, and schools.

Almost as soon as there were enough children in an area, a school would appear. The schools were fairly primitive by modern standards. Children learned reading, writing, and arithmetic, but little else. As soon as children were old enough to help on farms, they left school.

One man who was the son of a pioneer in South Dakota wrote about his school days. He remembered that each day he and his brother started for school. If any cattle were on the range between the farm and town, the boys turned back. This was because the cattle were half wild and very dangerous.

Another building likely to be found in these early towns was a church. The communities of farmers felt a need of religion in their lonely lives. When a pastor arrived, the whole community would pitch in to build a church. Everyone would help by bringing building materials or by spending time working on the building. These churches might be of one particular denomination, or of no denomination at all. Churches were a central part of any town and often formed the center of society.

Very different from the churches were the saloons. Some of these were wild drinking places where brawls were common. Many

more were simple, peaceful places where a farmer could meet his friends for a quiet drink. A few saloons were very grand. These were usually found in the larger towns. These saloons had stages and engaged actors and actresses to entertain the customers.

Throughout the closing years of the last century, the West saw a long parade of impressive stars. World famous singers and actors traveled by train to many towns in the West. Some theatrical companies even came from Europe to tour the West. Such visits may have been rare, but they provided great excitement in the farming communities.

The law found its first place in these towns. During the early days of the pioneers, law came from the barrel of a gun. It was only after farmers settled in large numbers that law and order could be enforced. Towns would elect sheriffs to enforce the law. Often these sheriffs were little better than the men they tried to keep in order.

Sometimes towns faced with a serious problem would deliberately hire a killer as sheriff. Only a hired gun would dare to try to impose law and order on a dangerous town. Such men as these created order in a town, often by shooting anybody who crossed them.

Usually, of course, sheriffs were respectable men. Their duties included locking up drunks and keeping an eye on young troublemakers. Only rarely did sheriffs have to tackle anything more dangerous.

The progress of the pioneer settlement from wagon train to peaceful town was a long one. Often the original pioneers were dead by the time a town came into existence. The part played by the pioneers was vital to America. They tamed a wilderness and made it a rich and fertile land. With sheer determination and courage these men and women carved a nation out of a wild country. The covered wagons and hard-working farmers have taken a rightful place in American history.

THE LAST PIONEERS

By 1890 the age of the pioneer seemed to be over. Only one more episode remained to be played. All of the West was taken up by farmers, ranchers or Indian reservations.

The largest reservation was that which covered the modern state of Oklahoma. The land was occupied by the tribes of the Cherokees, Creeks, Choctaws, Chicasaws and Seminoles. At the start of 1889, the tribes announced that they were willing to sell large

Everyone from far and wide would pitch in to help with the building of a church.

A street in Guthrie, a town which was settled in two and built in four days. The sheriff is ready to greet all newcomers.

areas of their reservation. The government bought nearly two million acres of land and prepared to open it up for settlement.

The government decided that the lands would be opened to pioneers at noon on April 22. Nobody would be allowed into the land before that time. Once the signal for settlement was given, people would be free to stake any piece of land they wanted. Each man would be able to claim 160 acres.

Word soon got around that there was free

This photograph is of the actual Oklahoma landrush in April, 1890.

land available. As April 22 approached, thousands of people arrived in Arkansas City, the official starting line for pioneers wishing to claim land. On April 19, the covered wagons rumbled forward towards unclaimed land. They moved out of Arkansas City towards the new lands.

Army scouts rode through the lands to be opened for settlement. They made sure that nobody had cheated and tried to claim land before April 22.

On the morning of April 22, soldiers under the command of Captain Hays of the 5th Cavalry were strung out along the border of the new lands. In front of them were thousands of people, all eager to claim farms. The soldiers were under orders to stop anybody passing them until Captain Hays signaled that it was noon.

The settlers had come from all over America. Some were in covered wagons. Others were mounted on fast horses, determined to be the first to the best land. A few were on foot, too poor to afford even a horse.

All through the morning the settlers waited

while tension mounted. At a few minutes to noon Captain Hays raised his hand in the air. Thousands of eyes were fixed on his arm. A deathly hush fell over the waiting crowds.

Suddenly Captain Hays dropped his hand. A great cheer went up from the settlers. They charged forwards, each man traveling as fast as he could. Within a single day, all the land had been claimed. Guthrie and Oklahoma City had been founded and the citizens had set up local government.

In 1893, another huge land rush took place. It was the end of an era for the pioneers of the West. Ever since the first wagons had creaked over the Oregon Trail in the 1840s there had been free land. Anybody who was adventurous enough to claim a farm could have one free.

Thousands of people had moved westward to look for a better life. They had faced incredible dangers. Settlers had traveled over vast distances. They carved farms out of a wilderness. Towns sprang up from nothing.

Now it was all over. There was no new land to settle. There were no free farms to claim. The age of the pioneers was over.

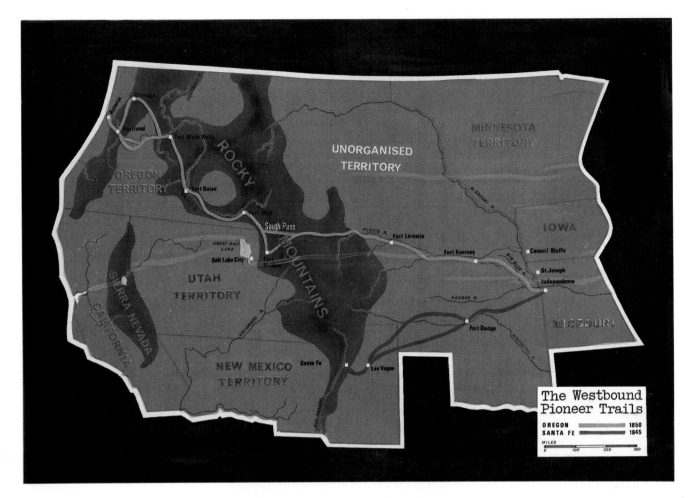

The Westbound
Pioneer Trails

OREGON ▬▬▬ 1850
SANTA FE ▬▬▬ 1845

MILES
0   100   200   300

PREPARATION

True grit! That is what anyone who wanted to be a settler in the untamed West had to have. True grit, for there would be months ahead when only the bravest of the brave could possibly hope to win through and reach their goal.

Those hardy pioneers who set out on the westward trails towards the rich and fertile lands knew and understood this. Imagine how brave they were, these sons and daughters of early America, and just think how the odds were stacked against their ever arriving at journey's end!

The pioneers had to cross a continent in wagons that they prayed would withstand the hardships of lumbering across endless miles of rocky ground. How they must have hoped that their horses and oxen would not fall ill or their wagons break down as they plodded across the vast prairies and toiled over high, snow-capped mountains.

How much warm clothing would they have to take? How many pairs of stout boots? How much food for the first few weeks before their hunters and scouts could shoot game to satisfy their hunger? What medical supplies? What guns? How much ammunition? All these questions and many more had to be answered, since they could make all the difference between life and death.

Apart from all the perils of wild, savage lands and harsh weather conditions, there were other dangers. These pioneers were, for the most part, honest, hard-working people who had saved the money they would need when they reached their "promised land." This hard-won cash was probably locked away in strong-boxes and stowed aboard the wagons, not to be opened until they were ready to settle down. This fact was known to the many bandit gangs that lined the trails, and the settlers had to be on constant watch for these killers. Their attacks were sudden and merciless.

Then, too, there were always the savage tribes of Indians — the Comanches, the Cheyennes, the Blackfeet and the Sioux. Sometimes these warriors could be bought off with a few trinkets or a horse or two. Even then they could not be trusted to let the wagons pass unhindered. The next day, at dawn, those same Indians, now painted for war, might well be creeping up unseen, bent on slaying every pioneer and making off with their wagons and cattle. From the Indians' point of view, they were defending their lands.

Even when the weary travelers had arrived at their destinations, they could be faced with bitter disappointment. For instance, several riders who took part in the Oklahoma land rush of April 22, 1889, were astonished to find that someone else had arrived there first. How had this happened? Several of those late arrivals knew that they had been ahead of the other riders. How could the plots they hoped for have already been staked out? Yet here were scowling men who, with guns ready, showed no sign of having ridden for miles and whose fresh horses were nibbling grass nearby.

The simple answer was that these gunmen were what were then called "sooners." They sneaked in

the night before, having successfully avoided the army sentries posted to guard against such crooked tricks. The sooners had planted their stakes. They were more than willing to prove their ownership of a particular piece of ground with the aid of their guns. In those hard days, possession was often worth more than nine-tenths of the law.

Looking back now, one wonders why it was that so many thousands of settlers set out in the first place. One reason was their dauntless spirit of high adventure, their courage to reach out and grasp the danger to improve their station in life. This spirit has always been a great part of the American nation.

Rough and tough were the lives of those early pioneers. Few people now could be tempted away from their mothers, their fathers, their comfortable homes, their cars, and their television sets, to set out on such dangerous adventures. Somehow, though, it seems sad that today nowhere in the world and never again can there be such another time or such opportunities offered to the young and brave in heart.

A Conestoga wagon

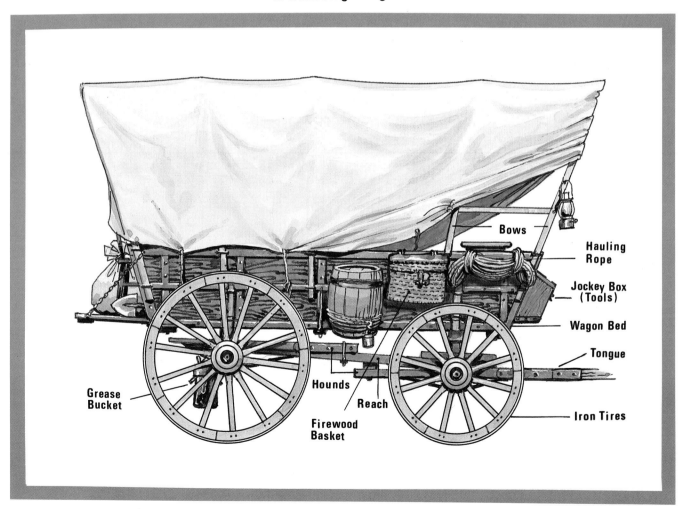

Bows

Hauling Rope

Jockey Box (Tools)

Wagon Bed

Tongue

Grease Bucket

Hounds

Reach

Iron Tires

Firewood Basket

IN THE DAYS OF THE PIONEERS

1492	Christopher Columbus discovers America.
1540-1542	Francisco Vasquez de Coronado explores the territory which is now New Mexico and Arizona. He is searching for seven fabled cities of gold to claim for Spain.
1669-1673	Rene Robert Cavelier (La Salle) becomes the first European to explore the Mississippi River to the Gulf of Mexico. He names it Louisiana, in honor of King Louis, and claims it for France.
1513	Vasco Nunez de Balboa becomes the first European to see the Pacific Ocean from what is now Panama. He claims Panama and the surrounding territory for Spain.
1690-1770	Texas and California become Spanish strongholds.
1776	The Declaration of Independence is signed.
1803	The U.S. buys Louisiana from France for $15,000,000.
1804	Meriwether Lewis and William Clark embark on the first expedition by the U.S. Government to explore the Northwest Territory.
1824-1830	Fur trappers arrive in the newly mapped Northwest Territory to hunt for pelts.
1775	Daniel Boone blazes the Wilderness Trail from North Carolina to Kentucky and founds Boonesborough, Kentucky.
1806	Zebulon Pike explores Colorado.
1825	The opening of the Erie Canal makes transportation to the west coast easier.
1849	Gold is discovered in California and the western rush is on.
1850	California becomes a state.
1850	New Mexico and Utah become territories.
1853	Washington becomes a territory.
1854	Kansas and Nebraska become territories.
1859	Oregon becomes a state.
1862	The Homestead Act gives 160 acres of western land to anyone who agrees to settle on it.
1867	Nebraska becomes a state.
1868	Wyoming is organized as a territory.
1876	Colorado becomes a state.
1889-1893	Treaties with Indians are ignored. Settlers flock to Indian lands in Oklahoma.
1892	Commodore Peary explores the Arctic.
1897	The discovery of gold in Alaska causes a rush to the Klondike.
1898	Hawaii is annexed to the U.S.